INERRANCY

You Better Learn This Word

George Shamblin

“

If we would destroy the Christian religion, we must first of all destroy man's belief in the Bible.

-- Voltaire, French philosopher and atheist (1694-1778)

”

Table of Contents

Introduction
My Commitment Moving Forward

The audience seated before me was as dialed in as any group I can ever recall. In my 20 years as a pastor, I'd never seen anything like it. Unfortunately, the occasion resulted from every parent's worst nightmare—a couple's 19-year-old son was killed by a drunk driver, and I was leading the funeral service. The family was broken, the friends were dismayed.

When the father of the deceased first called me, I could barely understand a word he said. Between his sobs, I could make out that the family wanted me to perform the funeral. I shared how sorry I was for what had happened and that I would be honored to help however I could. (Seminary gave me a lot, but how to preach a young person's funeral was something that couldn't be taught in a classroom.)

The family needed a pastor and to be comforted and consoled. But the one thing I knew they needed most was the spiritual food and drink freely offered to all who are hungry and thirsty, even if they're not quite sure what they're looking for—righteousness as offered by Jesus Himself, the Bread of Life and the Living Water. What they needed most was no different than what we all need in our respective mini or not so mini crises. Like the Greeks who approached Philip saying, "Sir, we wish to see Jesus" (John 12:21), we too must cry out "Sirs, we must see Jesus. We must see His word."

As family and friends gathered, I immediately noticed how young the crowd was. This was a wholly different generation that was raised on the superlatives. Their defining catch words and phrases were not in the middle but on the edges. Words like moderate, average, and normal were taboo, and in their place were words like extreme, radical, and awesome. As the crowd continued to pack the little chapel, I began to alter my sermon. I had been tipped off that this was an unchurched group and that I needed to keep it simple. That was easy. (After all, that's what all 40 authors of the Bible did.) But more than keeping it simple, I realized I needed to relay the extreme, radical, and awesome nature of the Gospel. Modern wisdom would have seen me tone it down for unchurched, hurting people. But the last thing this group needed was a run of the mill message filled with a whole lot of nothing. They needed more than trinkets and meaningless platitudes, and I wasn't about to patronize them with any of the all too popular "isms":

- They didn't need to be told just to be a good person and everything will be fine (moralism).

- They didn't need to be told that we are all going to heaven, just by different routes (universalism).

- They didn't need to be told to just believe and it will all work out (easy believism).

No—they needed to hear the unfiltered Word of God, the truth as it is in Jesus. They needed a reminder that they, too, would one day face the grave and must be ready to give an account for the hope they have (or the lack thereof). They needed the blood, sweat, and tears of the Cross of Christ, to understand where God was in the middle of their pain and suffering and loss. I assured them that He was in the same place at that moment as He was some 2,000+ years ago when His own Son exclaimed from the cross, "My God, My God why hast thou forsaken Me?" In both cases, He was seated on His throne, ruling for our good and His glory.

I can't remember whether it was during the beginning or the end of my time behind the pulpit at this funeral, but I sensed the Holy Spirit fanning into flames many dormant embers within me that had grown cold over time. After the service, I felt how I imagine so many marathon runners must feel when they cross the finish line—utter depletion mixed with a keen sense of fulfillment. I can't recall a time where I've preached with equal passion or zeal. When I preach today, I often think about that little chapel in Pensacola. I will never forget those puppy-like stares of perplexity that come from hearing the radical nature of the Gospel for the first time. I have no memory of a major revival within the hearts of those in attendance, but that's beyond the scope of the servant and wholly the matter of the Master. What I can say without a doubt is that I gave everything of myself to share God's Word with zero dilution or window dressing.

As a believer, many matters and mysteries are far beyond my reach. There's only so much I or anyone can do or control. But I don't want to stand before God one day trying to explain how His Word was forgotten during my time on earth only to be re-discovered again by later runners. Instead, we all should do what we've been entrusted by God to do—to feast on His Word and share the truth of the Good News with the world.

Chapter One
For Those Who Died in the Service

I believe that the Bible is 100% accurate, the miracles, the difficult to believe, and the seemingly contradictory—all of it. This belief is what's called biblical inerrancy, and it's at the heart of a massive debate defining modern Christianity. It's no different than the song from childhood that taught us to sing, "Jesus loves me this I know, for the Bible tells me so!"

Whether you already believe in biblical inerrancy or whether you're starting out as a skeptic like so many in the Church today, I invite you to stick with me for a quick assignment that will be eye opening. Simply ask any pastor or a pastor at your local church, without any preface, prompting, or clarification, whether or not they believe in inerrancy. Then sit back and listen.

If statistics bear true, a majority of pastors will preface their replies with "well...." or "it depends...." or avoid answering altogether by asking you a question. Even if their responses don't surprise you, their answers are incredibly important, because I believe the issue of inerrancy is the penultimate issue on which the Church will either stand or fall.

To emphasize inerrancy's importance and clear the air on what has caused so much confusion in the past, I'll share a few stories that have unfortunately become all too common in modern churches.

Can you recall an emphatic claim made by a minister that left you scratching your head, perhaps thinking, "Now wait a minute, that's not at all what the Bible says!"? Like the funeral I attended for an elderly fellow named Sam. The minister admonished us to rest assured, saying, "Sam's in a far better place, worshiping at present in the outstretched arms of Jesus." He made this statement even though Sam spared no insult to God, Jesus, and the Holy Spirit while He was alive. Later, the minister concluded by insisting that not only Sam, but all humankind, will arrive in Heaven through the pearly gates (i.e., universalism).

I am certainly not speaking to the status of Sam's salvation—that's between him and God, but the Bible couldn't be clearer when Christ warns, "Whoever is ashamed of Me and My words, the Son of Man will be ashamed of him." (Luke 9:26) or when Jesus teaches, "I am the door; if anyone enters through Me, he will be saved." (John 10:9)

Recently I ran into a dear friend of mine in the grocery store who's a long-time member of a local church. She'd been struggling. She couldn't quite put her finger on it, but something seemed off in the church. Come to find out, her church's leadership had recently advocated for a culturally relevant stance on something that quite clearly flew in the face of traditional, biblical teaching. While she knew in her gut something was off, my friend had no idea how to respond or what to believe.

When we find ourselves in the midst of churches and leadership who don't subscribe to biblical inerrancy, we can easily begin to second-guess all that we know to be true. How often do we hear, "Judge not, lest you be judged?" (Matthew 7:1) as a reason to accept something that runs counter to traditional, biblical truth? How quickly we also forget that, "You will know them by their fruits," (Matthew 7:16;20) appears shortly after in the same chapter. All of a sudden, we can begin to rationalize things that are counter to the truth, extending the benefit of the doubt to leaders who attended seminary and probably know more than us. All too easily, we forget that God's Word, not a pastor or church leadership's opinion, is the ultimate authority:

> "Beloved, do not believe every spirit, but test the spirits to see whether they are from God; because many false prophets have gone out into the world." (1 John 4:1)

The law of non-contradiction does not waver: A cannot be A and non-A at the same time and in the same sense. Inerrancy does not and cannot exist where the authority of the Bible is in question.

Christine Caine cautioned, "No weapon formed against you will prosper. But make no mistake, the weapon will be formed." And it has—the enemy's weapon of choice is confusion, as can be seen in the examples above and throughout the world today. What better way to mislead God's people than through the pulpit and church leadership? It's as terrifying as it is brilliant! As a result, pulpits are one of the enemy's most cherished platforms for broadcasting biblical distortions, misinformation, and untruths, and our churches have become memorials to all those who've died in their services.

In the pages that follow, I will share a few stories as well as some eye-opening statistics that all point to a common thread: again, biblical inerrancy is the issue on which the Church will stand or fall. Where inerrancy is ignored, humanity and the Church struggles. Where it is treasured, they thrive. I'm positive that this is no coincidence, and I hope you'll stick with me as we explore what I think is the most pressing issue currently facing the Church.

So, what do we do? If your pastor's response to the assignment I gave you at the beginning of this chapter was wavering, then my advice is straightforward: tie your shoelaces, because it's time for you to run. I say that because:

- Much like asking a pastor if they are a Christian or if they believe in Jesus, the question of biblical inerrancy is not one that requires clarification. A simple yes or no is all that's needed.
- Any pastor with a hint of biblical grounding realizes how they answer has major implications.
- If you don't come up with an immediate exit strategy for yourself and those under your care, you're poised to suffer a slow spiritual death by starvation, regardless of what service you attend.

This book isn't my attempt at a typical apologetics treatise designed to convince you with every possible argument or factual piece of evidence. The sheer amount of information would span multiple volumes, and to do so would take away from the basic premise of this book: there's power in seeking and finding answers for yourself.

Make no mistake, how you answer the question of biblical inerrancy will define your relationship with God and what your life looks like going forward.

Chapter Two
Cafeteria Christianity

During my senior year at Auburn University, my sister Ashley did the unthinkable—she married a Jesus Freak named Glenn. At the time, I thought that Jesus Freaks possessed the keen ability to suck the air out of a good time at a moment's notice. They weren't your run of the mill cultural Christians like the rest of us that were so typical in southern circles. They did things like talk about Jesus in public and quote the Bible in the company of genteel society. Back then, those types of actions felt like "needle scratch moments" to me, those awful screeching sounds record players make when the needle skips across the vinyl.

Don't get me wrong—I had been raised properly in the Deep South's Bible Belt. Sunday School, youth group, and church services were our routine, where we were strictly instructed that "all things must be done properly and with moderation." Bearing that in mind, to broach faith topics openly was excessive and went against the social norms of the day.

But Glenn's outspoken faith made me think hard. For the first time in my life, I reflected about matters pertaining to faith, and a single thought kept rotating in my mind like a hamster running tirelessly in its wheel: Is the Bible totally true or not?

The only place I could think to get an opinion was from the priest at Saint Dunstan's Episcopal Church. I can't recall a single topic we discussed that day, other than a specific question from me and a defining response from him. I asked whether or not the Bible is totally true. Without skipping a beat, he said, "Well, parts of it are true. Parts are untrue." I hadn't been trained in philosophy or theology, but I had enough common sense to ask the obvious: "How can you tell which is which?"

Like my priest at St. Dunstan's and the leadership in my friend's church and so many others, Thomas Jefferson thought that parts of the Bible were true and worth following and parts were not. But he went a step further and took it to its logical conclusion. In 1820, using razor and glue, he cut and pasted together a New Testament to his own liking. Jefferson's The Life and Morals of Jesus of Nazareth excluded all supernatural and miraculous references. Feeding the 5,000? Healing the lame? Walking on water? Turning water into wine? None of them made Jefferson's cut.

But the problem with this line of thinking is that man hasn't been afforded the wisdom to decide what God did or did not say in creating the Bible.

So, what are we to do?

The Bible was divinely inspired by God, but He used many different people over generations to write it.[i] In the natural world, it seems unlikely that it could ever withstand proper forensic analysis. It is much easier to believe the parts of the Bible that are palatable, but what about the passages in Scripture that seem awkward, contradictory, or difficult to believe? What about Jonah spending three days and nights in the belly of a fish, the flood and Noah's ark, or a literal devil being cast out of heaven like lightning? I'm the first to admit that many parts of the Bible seem hard to swallow, some rub me the wrong way, and some appear contradictory. But once you dismantle the parts, you've started a dangerous game of dismantling the whole—you will lose important context that helps the entire Bible make sense when looked at collectively.

Let's take Jesus of Nazareth for example. Almost everyone, regardless of beliefs, would universally agree that a historical figure named Jesus walked the earth 2,000 years ago. Even first century historical sources that are widely accepted today mention Jesus, including Josephus, Tacitus, and Pliny. (Whether or not they accepted Him as Messiah and a miracle worker is a different story that I invite you to research more in-depth.) Those sources are readily available and support a historical Jesus, but the bulk of what we know about Jesus Christ from 3 B.C. to 116 A.D. comes from the 27 books of the New Testament.

After doing my own research, I'm convinced there was no middle ground—Jesus was either who He says He was, fully God and fully Man and capable of the miraculous, or He was a lunatic fanatic. But don't just take my word for it—take a deeper look at the person of Jesus throughout the Bible as well as in available historical resources and come to your own conclusion. (I've included a brief appendix at the end of this book as a resource to help you get started.)

But how could someone as educated as Thomas Jefferson or a priest rely so heavily on the New Testament to prove Jesus' existence while also denying the Bible's reliability on the finer, miraculous details? (Jesus Himself believed and referenced Jonah, Noah's ark, and satan's[ii] fall from heaven.)[iii]

While we may struggle with these questions, they never caught Jesus off guard, this may explain why He warded off such objections with declarations like:

- "For whoever is ashamed of Me and *My words*, the Son of Man will be ashamed of him when He comes in His glory." (Luke 9:26)
- "It is written, 'man shall not live on bread alone, but on *every word* that proceeds out of the mouth of God.'" (Matthew 4:4)
- "If anyone loves Me, he will keep *My word*; and My Father will love him, and We will come to him and make Our abode with him. "He who does not love Me does not keep *My words*." (John 14:23-24)

Not once did Christ divide up His teachings into nice, neat categories for us to pick and choose based on how we feel. According to Jesus Himself, to believe in Him is to believe in all of Him and all that He said. He never left the door open for half measures.

> "If we are left in doubt as to which part is inspired and which is not, we are as badly off as if we had no Bible at all." – Charles Spurgeon[iv]

Biblical heroes, from Moses and David to Peter and Paul, embraced the teaching of inerrancy as foundational to everything they believed. It is the one thing, according to Isaiah, to exclusively outlive all else: "the grass withers, the flower fades, but the word of our God stands forever!" (Isaiah 40:8)

Unfortunately, the cafeteria plan approach to Christianity is gaining in popularity among trained, professional Christian leaders, the congregations they lead, and with many churchgoers. As a result, the united front of our faith has waned, leaving the body of Christ splintered.

I've also yet to find anyone who can give a satisfactory response to how you can tell which parts of the Bible are true and which are not. To evoke an ancient prophet:

> An appalling and horrible thing has happened in the land: The prophets prophesy falsely, and the priests rule on their own authority; And My people love it this way! But what will you do when the end comes? (Matthew 12:40-41)

This isn't some harmless, secondary side-note. As I've mentioned, it is the most important issue facing Christianity today. Fortunately, the path to recovery is clear, beginning and ending at the same place: reclaiming the doctrine of biblical inerrancy in its entirety.

Chapter Three
A Closer Look at Inerrancy: Why Should We Care?

For roughly 1,870 out of our 2,000+ year history,[v] most Christians around the world viewed the Bible as accurate, or inerrant. In fact, inerrancy was a view held by Church Fathers, medieval Christian leaders, and the Reformers. (It wasn't until Johan Semler in 1779 that we saw the first serious challenge to inerrancy arise.)[vi]

Looking more in-depth at the term, we learn that inerrancy means:

- **The Bible tells us the truth:**
  "Your word is truth..." (John 17:17)
  "These words are trustworthy and true." (Revelation 22:6)

- **God is honest and unable to lie:**
  "It is impossible for God to lie." (Hebrews 6:18)

- **God communicates through Scripture:**
  "When you received the word of God which you heard from us, you accepted it not as the word of mere men, but as what it really is, the word of God." (1 Thessalonians 2:13)

- **Prophets didn't make things up based on their feelings:**
  "For prophecy never had its origin in the human will, but prophets, though human, spoke from God as they were carried along by the Holy Spirit." (2 Peter 1:21 NIV)

- **The Bible isn't littered with filth, impurities, or imperfections:**
  "Your word is very pure, therefore your servant loves it." (Psalm 119:140) "The Law of the Lord is perfect!" (Psalm 19:7)

Only over the last 150 years or so did the above positions come under attack. But why should we care? What difference does it make in our modern world?

Practically

We should care about inerrancy because it's the only math that adds up, which reminds me of a funny story about President Lyndon Johnson's nephew, Randy, who once quarterbacked Oklahoma State's football team.

In the final game of their season, they found themselves on their own 20-yard-line, trailing rival Oklahoma by six points with only 8 seconds remaining. With little hope of scoring, their coach put in all his seniors for the last play of the game, telling his 3rd-string quarterback Randy to call whatever play he wanted.

Randy called play 13, a trick play they'd never used (it'd never even worked in practice!). But the impossible happened, and Oklahoma State scored, winning the game by one point. The fans carried Randy off the field, who then told his coach why he called play 13:

> Well, we were in the huddle, and I looked over and saw old Harry with tears running down his cheeks. It was his last college game and we were losing. And I saw that big 8 on his chest. Then I looked over and saw Ralph. And tears were running down his cheeks, too. And I saw that big 7 on his jersey. So in honor of those two heartbroken seniors, I added eight and seven together and called play 13!

His coach mentioned the obvious, that eight and seven don't add up to 13. Randy reflected for a minute and said, "You're right, coach! And if I'd been as smart as you are, we would have lost the game!"[vii]

While Randy Johnson may have gotten away with bad math, our society and culture cannot. A quick look around at our societal decay makes that abundantly clear. If the world's solutions to life are so smart, and the Bible is so antiquated and wrong, why do so many followers of Jesus have peace amidst the world's chaos?

Theologically

We should care about inerrancy because God made a really big deal about it in the 66 letters He wrote to us. Think about that for a second—God wrote to us! I don't mean to sound snarky, but that means He cares, and so should we. To discover His feelings on the subject, simply search for expressions like "My word; My Law;

My statutes, My commands" in a Bible app and see what God has to say.

Culturally

We should care about inerrancy because our culture is drifting. Everybody knows it, but we're unable to agree on the best way to navigate our way back to solid ground.

This reminds me of a family vacation I took to Kiawah Island in the early 90s. My brother-in-law Glenn flew one-way, because he intended to ride home in a car with my brother Keith and talk about Jesus with him along the way. Before they drove home, an excellent opportunity for evangelism presented itself. As Glenn and Keith floated on a raft in the Atlantic, Glenn said, "Keith, we've been on this raft talking for ten minutes, oblivious to how far the current has pulled us in such a short amount of time." Glenn pointed to their chairs and umbrella on the shore for reference. The distance they'd traveled surprised Keith, and Glenn continued, "Unless you're immersed in God's Word, you wouldn't even notice how far you've drifted. Like in Psalm 119:9, that says 'How can a young man keep his way pure? By keeping it according to Thy word.'"

Similarly, to stop the cultural and societal drift we're experiencing and work our way back to shore, we must first moor ourselves to an anchor that's immovable. Only Christ and His infallible word are steadfast in the face of shifting tides and heavy storms. He alone is safe and secure, the "Anchor of the soul."[viii] Once fastened to Christ, we can then regain our bearings.[ix]

Factually

We should care about biblical inerrancy because it is the sole issue from which all current cultural, social, and theological divides in Christianity flow.

> "The Scriptures are either the infallible, inerrant Word of God, or they are 'good suggestions for decent living.'"
> – Pastor Steve Singletary

It's one or the other, and if followers of Christ can't agree on which is true, all attempts at settling internal disputes or posing a united front to the outside world become obsolete.

The Mighty Mississippi

Picture biblical inerrancy as the rapidly flowing Mississippi River. As we travel downstream, there would seem to be no end to the number of offshoots from the main channel. There are hundreds, if not thousands, of small streams, marshes, creeks, tributaries, etc. Similarly, in a theological framework, the offshoots of inerrancy can look like the following:

- What is the church's position on climate change?
- Do church politics alienate the people we're trying to reach?
- Should worship be online or in person?
- Does my church turn a blind eye to members living together without being married?
- How does my church handle generational divides?
- Should my church lean Democrat or Republican?
- Should my church address politics from the pulpit?
- What's my church's stance on social issues?
- Is Jesus a way to heaven, or *the* only way?
- Is my church pro-life or pro-choice?
- What's my church's position on gender and human sexuality?
- Where does my church stand on same-sex marriage?

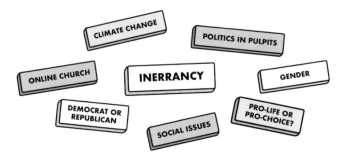

Unfortunately, churches keep entangling themselves down river, while what ultimately needs addressing lies at the source. While all of these hot-button topics are tremendously significant and must be addressed in due time, we have zero chance of resolving them until agreement is reached on biblical inerrancy.

As the Church, we can't afford to be like the passengers on a sinking cruise ship who are more concerned about the dress code and what's being served in the luxury dining hall than the holes below the water line. None of it will be settled unless we start at the source, and unity in the body of Christ will be non-existent until consensus on biblical authority is reached.

"If you look at it this way, it's not that bad."

Chapter Four
The Numbers Game

Christian organizations in America are captivated by numbers, yet they can be deceptive, especially in matters of faith. We love to ask, "how big is your church?" as if that were the sole factor for determining the health of a church. It is certainly wise for denominations and churches and para-church ministries to review and consider all sorts of numbers to see if blind spots exist or if any blaring shortcomings need to be overcome, but numbers alone don't tell the whole story.

While excellence in whatever we put our hand to is an essential biblical principle, many variables must be considered when assessing effectiveness for the Kingdom of God. For instance, a temporary increase in membership for one church could have its roots in a negative source, whereas a decrease in membership for another may have its roots in something positive.

Is it really a good thing if a church quickly doubles attendance from 500 to 1,000 by dumbing down the message or conceding the inerrancy of Scripture on a cultural hot topic? Of course not. Even a dusty circus can scare up a big crowd. But if names fill the church rolls without ultimately being recorded in the Lamb's Book of Life, what's the point?

> "If you have to give a carnival to get people to come to church, then you will have to keep giving carnivals to keep them coming back."
>
> – Charles Spurgeon

Fully intent to preach "unpopular" messages, Spurgeon also told his fellow ministers that, "You have to preach them out before you can preach them in." Some of his messages even referenced that he believed many churchgoers were unthinking, slumbering worshippers of an unknown God. No doubts lingered as to the future direction of Metropolitan Tabernacle Church under Spurgeon's leadership. Be it high numbers or low, Scripture's supremacy would reign. As providence would have it, history's "prince of preachers" is the most quoted and referenced minister in history.

Please remember that with dedication to the truth comes a responsibility to fulfill the Great Commission. We certainly can't ignore the truth according to Scripture, but we must remember to gracefully pour God's truth into the lives of others. While *grace without truth* can lead to a weak, pick-and-choose Christianity, *truth without grace* can be downright mean. Salt should perfectly season truthful speech, and a winsome attitude will almost always win. Just look at Jesus' interactions with people during His life and ministry. He proved that truth can and should be cloaked in grace!

Numbers Can Be Tricky

Nowhere is our fascination with numbers more obvious than the predictable superlatives and accolades used to introduce so many Christian celebrities. At the next conference you attend, keep your ear open for any of the following:

- "So and so is a **very successful** Pastor."

It's interesting how "very" gets emphasized. How are they defining success, much less quantifying it? "Successful" and "pastor" in the same sentence continually strikes me as odd!

- "The church continues to **thrive** under so and so's leadership"

This has become a habitual favorite, and yet I still can't figure out by what metrics we are measuring a church's ability to thrive.

- "**His church** has **outgrown** the last few **buildings**..."

This is most irksome of all and is a sentence containing as many errors as it does words. Jesus claimed the Church was His, not ours. The second-person pronoun "His" in conjunction with "church" better be capitalized, because the declaration of ownership belongs exclusively to the Second Person of the Trinity.

What impressed Jesus?

It's worth asking what might the World's Savior emphasize should He introduce a servant of His? "Successful," I suppose, wouldn't be out of the question; although our definitions of what constitutes success would vary greatly. "He who trembles at My word" seems, at least to me, closer to the mark. If I were to circle my best guess,

27

I'd have to go with: "what does The Lord require of you: but to do what is right, to love mercy, and to walk humbly with your God." (Micah 6:8)

It is the humble man who knows his place when stacked up against Scripture. Who is he to question, "Why is it so?" to His God? Who is he to help God better articulate what needs to be said? The humble man's highest ideal is neither numbers nor a great name for himself, but excellence in whatever he does. At the top of his list is loyalty to God's Word, and from it he will never sway.

> "If you should ask me what are the ways of God, I would tell you that the first is humility, the second is humility, and the third is humility. Not that there are no other instructions to give, but if humility does not proceed all that we do, our efforts are fruitless."
> – Augustine of Hippo

As we've seen, judging church growth can be tricky business. On one end of the spectrum, you have churches obsessed with numbers. On the other end, you've got churches who say they don't matter at all. The truth lies between them both, and Jesus is our best example. By contemporary growth models, Jesus would have easily flunked. Instead of shining a spotlight on the miracles He performed, He shied attention away from it, knowing the public would try and force Him to take an earthly throne. He often said, "Go and tell no one!" Jesus didn't boast about packing a synagogue to capacity or having to add an overflow room whenever He preached. This was quite the departure from our habitual mass-marketing.

On the far-opposite side would be the dying or non-thriving churches waving the "numbers don't matter" banner, which is often a cliché shared among churches in decline. However, The New Testament would beg to differ; it applauds churches for greater numerical reach into their communities. In Acts 16:5, Luke wrote, "The churches were being strengthened in the faith, and were *increasing in number* daily." In Acts 5:14, he wrote, "And all the more believers in the Lord, multitudes of men and women, were constantly *added to their number*."

Luke didn't hesitate to connect causes and effects for his readers. According to him, increased conversions went hand-in-hand with sound teaching, like when "nearly all the city assembled to hear the word of the Lord" preached by Paul and Barnabas, after which time the Gentiles "began rejoicing and glorifying the word of the Lord; and all who had been appointed to eternal life believed. And the word of the Lord was being spread through the whole region."(Acts 13:48) Seeing converts as a direct result of sound teaching might not always equate, but there is a connection. Regardless, praise God anytime pews overflow due to "an unashamed workman who accurately handles the word of truth!" (2 Timothy 2:15 BSB)

Jesus was intent on numbers, but not in the way we so commonly frame them today. His ultimate concern? Adding names to the Lamb's Book of Life. Jesus was clear: If it meant leaving the 99 sheep temporarily to go retrieve one more? Then so be it. If it took hitting the highways and hedges that His house may be filled? Then let it be done. But Jesus never watered down the truth to make it more appealing— neither should we.

"Well, at least he tells it like it is."

Chapter Five
Smoke and Mirrors

As Leslie Millstead reached her mid-forties, she couldn't recall missing church on consecutive Sundays in the small Georgia town where she was raised. Her church was the picturesque kind you might envision occupying a prominent corner in the heart of a small, rural downtown.

One Thanksgiving, as was the family custom, Leslie and her children, siblings, parents, and grandparents filled the third, fourth, and fifth row pews on the left side of the sanctuary. Seats weren't assigned back then, but there was a common understanding amongst parishioners, that these seats might as well have been marked by a sign saying, "don't sit there, that's where the Millsteads sit."

The worship service had hardly changed at all over the years. You could practically set your watch by what would take place and when. Things had always been done a certain way and would continue to do so. However, with the subtle insertion of a single preposition by the new pastor, and I do mean a single preposition, Leslie's lifelong familiarity with her church home and church family was upended.

As the Pastor settled behind the pulpit, he signaled for the entire congregation to rise and hear the Bible reading for that day's sermon, a tradition practiced since the church's inception. The point of standing was to signify a high level of awe and respect at the public reading of God's Word. He further instructed, "Listen for the word of God," and proceeded to recount the selected portion of Scripture.

As everyone took their seats, something didn't sit right with Leslie. She had a feeling in her gut, a discernment that something was off. As she silently replayed the Pastor's words in her head, it finally clicked, "Listen for the word of God....Listen *for* the word of God... Listen for the word of God..." Instead of "Listen *to* the word of God," as so many preachers before had affirmed, this pastor altered that one preposition, and it made all the difference.

> "Discernment is not knowing the difference between right and wrong. It is knowing the difference between right and almost right."
> – Charles Spurgeon

Fortunately, Leslie had just returned from a women's conference where the subject of biblical inerrancy came up. While she had never heard the word before, she had great respect for the speaker who warned about the sneaky subtleties and nuances surrounding it.

So what difference does the small change of prepositions make? If you are someone who believes the entirety of the Bible is true, or if you or someone you care about attends one of the many denominations currently making this distinction, that one tiny change can help you to understand why the membership rolls of so many churches and denominations have been hemorrhaging for decades.

This shift in outlook has its roots in the eighteenth century and the father of modern liberal theology, German theologian and biblical scholar Friedrich Schleiermacher. He spent his life attempting to reconcile criticisms of the Enlightenment with traditional Protestant Orthodox Christianity. During his studies, he became increasingly skeptical and ultimately rejected Orthodox Christianity. At the University of Halle, he even attacked the Bible as being totally corrupt.

As strange as it may seem, Schleiermacher's approach, along with his like-minded contemporaries, was less destructive than Karl Barth's, another prominent theologian who followed on their heels. Schleiermacher and his contemporaries' hostility towards Scripture was blatant. It left no room for interpretation, ultimately leaving their ultra-radical objections open for easier discreditation.

Barth's angle, on the other hand, was subtle and serene. While I believe much of the time he was well-intentioned, he left greater damage in his wake. If Schleiermacher and company swung the pendulum to the extreme left, Barth swung it subtly and dangerously back to the inerrancy-conceding middle.

"I do not think the devil cares how many churches you build, if you only have lukewarm preachers and people in them."

– Charles Spurgeon

Barth insisted that the Bible is not the word of God, but rather that it merely *contains* the word of God. According to him, believers are tasked with listening *for* it rather than *to* it. It's a subtle distinction, and it's easy to miss if you're not paying attention. What it means is that Barth believes parts of the Bible are true and parts are untrue, and it's up to readers to sort out which is which. (Interestingly enough, neither Barth nor the pastors who promote his neo-orthodoxy teachings can explain exactly how that's done.)

Regardless, an unbridgeable chasm exists between what Barth said about the Bible and what the Bible says about itself (emphasis mine):

- "*Every* word of God is flawless." (Proverbs 30:5 NIV)

- "*All* Scripture is inspired by God." (2 Timothy 3:16)

- "*All* His precepts are sure." (Psalm 111:8)

- "The judgments of the Lord are true; they are righteous *altogether*." (Psalm 19:9)

Unfortunately, much of Karl Barth's teachings have influenced many seminaries and infiltrated the hearts and minds of numerous preachers over the last two centuries. We now find ourselves living in a world where there is no guarantee that a Christian preacher believes the entirety of the Bible.

Death by Incrementalism

Have you ever noticed how the fastest dying institutions are the ones making the most concessions? (Just look at the Boy Scouts of America, whose collapse is unfolding right in front of us.) The same principle applies to churches and denominations across the world, especially those that classify themselves as Barthian (i.e., they prescribe to Karl Barth's theology about the Bible.). They have fooled themselves into thinking, "If we bend a tiny bit here," or "If we concede a sliver there," then all will be well and that they could even grow the size of their congregations. But at what cost?

Compromise is a slippery slope. Once one is made, the next becomes easier, and so on. When churches pick and choose where to draw the line, they will eventually find themselves having conceded principle after principle to the point that their original reason for existence is left behind.

Raymond Brown said it best:

> All too easily, an ugly thing becomes tolerated, even viewed as the possibly useful thing, then the permissible thing, and finally the attractive thing. It does not

happen in a moment. Standards are lowered gradually and imperceptibly. Sin becomes known by another name. We accommodate at one stage of life things which earlier would have been totally unacceptable.

Show me a loose-leaning, enlightened church that's seen its membership leave in droves, and I'll show you a Bible-believing church in the same area that's growing by leaps and bounds. Anecdotally, this describes exactly what happened at Leslie Millstead's church. Unfortunately, as Leslie's pastor would have it, the issue of inerrancy remained unsettled. Like a magician dependent on smoke to divert the attention of his audience and mirrors to create illusions, he refused to disclose where his true intentions lay. Church membership dwindled because people were starving to hear right versus wrong, either a yes or a no. The Bible is clear, and we should be, too!

Maybes have grown grossly out of style, and relativism has appeared to run its course. I don't think this should come as a surprise—we are hard-wired for boundaries, only resting securely when we know where those boundaries lie. A Bible without a clear distinction between yes and no, do and don't, isn't a Bible at all.

> "The glory of the gospel is that when the church is absolutely different from the world, she invariably attracts it. It is then that the world is made to listen to her message, though it may hate it at first. That is how revival comes."
>
> – Pastor Martyn Lloyd-Jones

Is there really much to find attractive in a theology like Barth's that agrees with a worldview of relativistic truth? God had a purpose in calling His people out from among others. Just as the Israelites in the Old Testament, Christians are called by God to stand out from the crowd and influence it for God's Kingdom, not the other way around.

Reverend Fred Holloman, chaplain of the Kansas Senate, led an insightful prayer before an opening session of the legislature:

> Omniscient Father: Help us to know who is telling the truth. One side tells us one thing, and the other just the opposite. And if neither side is telling the truth, we would like to know that, too. And if each side is telling half the truth, give us the wisdom to put the right halves together. In Jesus' Name, Amen.

The Bible is either 100% true or it isn't. Do not assume your pastor or church leaders believe the entire Bible is true. When we blindly think that their default is one of biblical inerrancy, we are playing a dangerous game with who and what we allow to speak into our lives with spiritual authority. Maintain a healthy attitude of skepticism toward anyone and any institution that is promoting beliefs that run counter to the Bible—you'll be glad you did.

Chapter Six
A Crack in the Door

I once heard a story about a lonely woman who bought a parrot to keep her company. Disappointed that the parrot wouldn't talk, she returned to the pet store. The store suggested she buy the parrot a ladder to walk on. She did, but the parrot still wouldn't talk. The next day she returned to the store, where they recommended she buy fluffy toys for her parrot to play with. That didn't work either, and finally the woman's parrot died. When she told the pet store, they asked if it ever said a word. "Yes, right before it died," the woman said, "it asked if they sold food at that pet store!"

I believe the answer for the mass exodus of parishioners from so many mainline Christian denominations is simple. They're leaving because they are starving and want to be fed with truth. Do we really need to stray from the sanctity of God's Word to try and attract new attendees? Or to form another sub-committee to study the problem of why masses have already left? Are a wave of trinkets and shiny new toys really going to increase retention?

Why not learn a lesson from the woman with the parrot: Just be like Jesus and give them something to eat!

"Do not work for the food that perishes, but for the food that lasts for eternal life, which the Son of Man will give you, for on Him the Father, God, has set His seal." (John 6:27)

"Jesus said to them, 'I am the bread of life; the one who comes to Me will not be hungry, and the one who believes in Me will never be thirsty.'" (John 6:35)

Now, imagine you inherited a sixth or seventh-generation bakery that thrived for decades prior to your time in charge. In the late nineteenth century and throughout most of the twentieth, the growing success of the organization seemed boundless. Along with steady year-to-year profits, your family-owned business provided abundantly for the livelihood of scores of employees and their families.

But things changed when you took over in 1966. Astonishingly, for the next 56 years under your leadership (1966-2022), revenue decreased every year. Your once-thriving bakery has shrunk to a shell of its former self. Annual revenue in 1966 was $4.25 million. Today it is a depressing $1.2 (72% decrease). What's worse? The amount of people dependent upon your bakery has increased exponentially over the same time period, and your customer base has increased 66%.[x]

More people are dependent upon your bakery, which is failing and unable to support the needs of its employees and the community which it serves. As a business owner whose livelihood depends on the bakery's success, wouldn't it make sense for you to take a good look in the mirror and figure out what in the world you're doing wrong?

While a similar scenario plays itself out across so many denominations throughout the United States, it is all too real and mirrors what has happened to the largest Presbyterian denomination in the United States, the Presbyterian Church USA (PCUSA). Can you fathom! Since 1966, their membership has decreased for 56 consecutive years, that's 56 years in a row of losses—seriously? From a high of 4.25 million members in 1966, to 1.2 today. During that same period, the population of the United States grew 66%, from 201 million to 334 million.[xi]

The PCUSA's top spokesman, Rev. Dr. J. Herbert Nelson, said, "We are not dying...we are reforming." His solution to the problem? "For the first time in more than thirty years, the PCUSA is not reporting membership losses," he cheered. "Our membership remains at 1.3 million. This is good news! We must celebrate while knowing that there remains work to be done."[xii]

Incidentally, membership has dropped an additional 15.63% since that statement was released on May 24, 2017.[xiii]

For me, the biggest conundrum is trying to decide which is worse, preventative measures like the PCUSA simply choosing not to report their losses, or prescriptive solutions at the local level, like a PCUSA church with which I am familiar. When their college-aged students quit attending church, leadership opted to integrate show tunes into the service to woo them back. College students and show tunes? *Talk about tone-deaf!* God's Word offers a far simpler solution: "Observe my Sabbaths and have reverence for my sanctuary; I am the Lord!" (Leviticus 19:30)

But how did the PCUSA find itself in such decline? I believe it started with a watershed moment in May 1924, when 1,274 Presbyterian pastors signed the Auburn Affirmation, which challenged the right of the body of the church to impose Five Fundamentals as a test of orthodoxy.

The Five Fundamentals were like a litmus test, and every candidate seeking to be ordained in the Presbyterian Church should be able to affirm:

1. Inerrancy of the Scriptures
2. The virgin birth (and the deity of Jesus)
3. The doctrine of substitutionary atonement
4. The bodily resurrection of Jesus
5. The authenticity of Christ's miracles

The Auburn Affirmation, among other things, concluded that the Bible is *not* inerrant and that *none* of the Five Fundamentals listed above should be used as a test of ordination.

Can you imagine a pastor leading a Presbyterian Church who did not believe in the deity of Jesus Christ, the virgin birth, the bodily resurrection of Jesus, and the belief in His miracles! As more and more church leaders and pastors agreed with the Auburn Affirmation and the denial of biblical inerrancy, it's no wonder the PCUSA has been in steady decline since the 1960s.

It would be misleading to suggest that the PCUSA stands alone in denying the sufficiency of Scripture. Tally up the mainline churches plus a whole host of others who have shifted away from inerrancy, and we are looking at a majority of American churches.

But this shouldn't come as a surprise. During the first half of the twentieth century, Francis Schaeffer predicted this downfall.

> "Any denomination or church group that forsakes inerrancy will end up shipwrecked. It is impossible to prevent the surrender of other important doctrinal teachings of the Word of God when inerrancy is gone."
> – Francis Schaeffer

It's no coincidence that the collective losses of many American churches coincides with a departure from the belief in Scripture's authority over the last century. Too many mistruths have originated from too many pastors and church leaders for far too long, but the complicity of millions of churchgoers week-in and week-out shouldn't be overlooked. Which of us voiced objections to sermons questioning the authority of God's Word on a subject? Which of us pulled a preacher aside to ask questions about their methods or an apparent falsehood? What about our children? Could their apathy toward God and Jesus be a behavior they learned from us or the church they attend?

These questions are good to ask, but they are only as effective as we are willing to act upon the answers we receive. Cafeteria Christianity and biblical relativism are dangerous—but are we willing to walk away from what's been comfortable in favor of what's best, even if it asks more of us?

Al Mohler, theologian and current President of The Southern Baptist Theological Seminary, shared about the ongoing battle surrounding biblical inerrancy and its importance:

> Back in 1990, theologian J. I. Packer recounted what he called a "Thirty Years' War" over the inerrancy of the Bible. He traced his involvement in this war in its American context back to a conference held in Wenham, Massachusetts in 1966, when he confronted some professors from evangelical institutions who "now declined to affirm the full truth of Scripture." That was nearly fifty years ago, and the war over the truthfulness of the Bible is still not over—not by a long shot.
>
> From time to time, the dust has settled in one arena, only for the battle to erupt in another. In the 1970s, the most visible battles were fought over Fuller Theological Seminary and within the Lutheran Church—Missouri Synod. By the 1980s, the most heated controversies centered in the Southern Baptist Convention and its seminaries. Throughout this period, the evangelical movement sought to regain its footing on the doctrine. In 1978, a large number of leading evangelicals met and adopted a definitive statement that became known as "The Chicago Statement on Biblical Inerrancy."

Many thought the battles were over, or at least subsiding. Sadly, the debate over the inerrancy of the Bible continues. As a matter of fact, there seems to be a renewed effort to forge an evangelical identity apart from the claim that the Bible is totally truthful and without error.[xiv]

The numbers don't lie, and they can be discouraging if we aren't careful. But it reminds me of a time a guy was driving home from work one day. He stopped to watch a local little league baseball game at a park near his home. As he sat behind the bench on the first-base line, he asked one of the boys for the score.

"We're behind fourteen to nothing," he said with a smile.

"Really," he said. "I have to say you don't look very discouraged."

"Discouraged?" the boy asked with puzzled look on his face. "Why should we be discouraged? We haven't been up to bat yet."

None of this is new. The enemy has crouched on the steps outside of Gospel churches from Paul's day until now. He sits poised and ready to kick open the door at the slightest sign of a crack. Countless have fallen prey to his schemes of having us question Scripture's integrity, and he's not about to retreat. No Christian, pastor, church, or denomination can afford to stray from the authority of God's Word even in the slightest.

But be encouraged, Bible-believers! We have inherited the true bread out of heaven, with plenty to go around. Recent history may be bent towards those espousing pick-and-choose Christianity, and we may have ceded large tracts of sacred ground. But now is our time to step up to the plate and go to bat to reclaim the inerrancy of God's Word!

THEIR CHANGING!
OUR ONLY CHOICE
IS TO CHANGE
WITH THEM!

MR. EXECUTIVE

Chapter Seven
Nothing Compares to the Real Thing:
New Methodism vs. the Original

In 1985, a famous beverage enjoyed the world over for nearly a century faced its most formidable challenge. After years and years of dominating the industry, some felt Coca-Cola had lost its edge, appearing old and outdated, unable to compete in an increasingly diverse market. A rival-brand had also encroached on its territory by conducting nationwide taste tests. Overwhelmingly, participants chose the challenger brand over the reigning champion.

On April 23 of that same year, after investing $4 million in research and conducting taste tests of their own, corporate executives took a gamble by yanking their staple, Coca-Cola, and replacing it with New Coke, a sweeter, bolder version of the original. The negative response from consumers was immediate. Within days, Coca-Cola's corporate mailrooms were flooded with 400,000 letters of objection. In protest, bottles and cans of New Coke were poured into Seattle's sewers, and its ads were booed out of Houston's Astrodome. New Coke is now remembered as one of the biggest flops in American merchandising history.

The story of New Coke is a cautionary tale against tampering with a well-established and successful brand. As crazy as it sounds, the New Coke experiment mirrors what took place in American Methodism in more ways than you might expect.

Starting in 1729, the tiny Methodist movement at Oxford University grew over two centuries to what is now considered the gold standard by which subsequent revivals are measured. But by the 1960s, clergy and many seminaries, much like the executives at Coca-Cola, felt the denomination had lost its edge, appearing old and outdated, unable to gain traction in increasingly modern minds. With that, the old-timey religion went out, the new and improved version came in. The denomination's growth has waned ever since.

But, much like the story of New Coke, tremendous change for the better can still occur. What was true with Coca-Cola may prove true with other institutions, especially considering there is more to the Coca-Cola story than recounted above. Once executives returned to the original, Coca-Cola experienced an epic return to prominence. But before considering the plausibility of a comeback from biblical relativism, I think it's important to take a quick look at Methodist history, including the denomination's creation, climb, collapse, and prospective comeback.

Creation
The four students comprising the first "Holy Club" conceived on Oxford University's campus in 1729 would hardly have fit the bill

as eventual household names. Little that took place in their regular meetings was necessarily new or extraordinary: they had no new teachings to espouse, no new theologies to expound upon. However, what they did possess was an unflinching zeal "for the very things of God" at a time when religiosity was on the outs.

They were maligned by fellow students as fanatics, Bible Moths, Bible Bigots, and "Methodists" as characterized by their strict adherence to "methods." One might naturally assume they were religious rabble-rousers. In fact, their seemingly great offense stemmed from living disciplined, godly lives that included receiving communion weekly, holding nightly devotions, ministering to prisoners and the sick, fasting until 3:00 p.m. on Wednesdays and Fridays, and holding one another accountable. Hardly condemnable crimes.

The Climb

The Holy Club's membership never surpassed 25 students on Oxford's campus, but the groundswell of influence that began there reverberated globally for centuries to come. By the time of founding member John Wesley's death in 1791, 132,000 people from the British Isles and America declared themselves Methodists. By 1840, the Methodists were the largest denomination in America, overtaking the reigning colonial denominations: Presbyterians, Congregationalists, and Anglicans. By 1968, the membership rolls of the United Methodist Churches tallied nearly 11 million.

Any time an organization climbs from four people to 25 to 132,000 and then to nearly 11 million, it would be foolish not to attribute such exponential growth to someone or something. Rather than rely on guesswork, direct references from founder John Wesley himself reveal his thoughts on the subject:

I want to know one thing,—the way to heaven; how to land safe on that happy shore. God himself has condescended to teach me the way. For this very end He came from heaven. He hath written it down in a book. O give me that book! At any price, give me the book of God! I have it: here is knowledge enough for me. Let me be [a man of one book].[xv]

As for that "one book," Wesley removed all doubt about how much of it he viewed as authoritative:

The Scripture, therefore, of the Old and New Testaments is a most solid and precious system of divine truth. Every part thereof is worthy of God; and all together are one entire body, wherein is no defect, no excess. It is the fountain of heavenly wisdom which they who are able to taste prefer to all writings of men, however wise or learned, or holy.[xvi]

Collapse

It's been said that churches, like those who attend them, don't fall into sin, they slide. By the same token, institutions don't collapse in a day, they decay over time. United Methodist membership counts in the United States have declined each year from 1968 to present day: down from 10,990,720 in its heyday to 6,268,310 million today, almost a 43% decrease.[xvii, xviii]

What could have caused such a dramatic reversal of fortunes? Unsurprisingly, the answer once again is my reason for writing this book: Methodism's decay began when they abandoned their first love, Holy Scripture.

Mark Tooley provided a reason that I agree with in an article written for the Institute on Religion & Democracy:

> Why did Methodist decline start 50 years ago? Here's my theory. Methodism's official seminaries were all captured by liberalism by the 1920s. Most clergy weren't seminary trained until mid century, but the course of study materials for non-seminary trained clergy closely followed seminary curricula. By the 1960s nearly all of the clergy would have been trained in theological modernism, denying or minimizing the supernatural and personal salvation in favor of Social Gospel and therapeutic themes.[xix]

Consider the following:

- A 1963 survey of church members shows that only 34% of United Methodists believe that "Jesus was born of a virgin" and is "completely true." Yet this truth is at the very heart of the gospel itself! Interestingly, the "Baptismal Covenant" of the United Methodist Church requires the candidate to answer affirmatively, "I believe in Jesus Christ, his only Son, our Lord, [who was conceived by the Holy Spirit, born of the Virgin Mary. . . .]."[xx]

- By 1971, only 18% of Methodists believed in "a literal or nearly literal interpretation of the Bible," and only 13% believed the "Scriptures are the inspired and inerrant Word of God not only in matters of faith but also in historical, geographical and other secular matters."[xxi]

In other words, the theological decay that started in the 1960s and 1970s led to the mess the UMC finds itself in today. It seems obvious, but if Methodism's global expansion was due to their strict adherence to Scripture, why would modern churches abandon the thing responsible for their success in the first place? To me, it's mind-boggling how this question is so often overlooked.

Comeback

Who doesn't love a comeback story? Less than three months into the New Coke debacle, the company's executives relented to public pressure and brought back the original formula, renamed "Coca-Cola Classic." The reception was overwhelming. It turned out to be a brilliant move; within weeks Coke reclaimed massive amounts of market share. In the end, what had seemed like a complete disaster turned into a success story. Perhaps the best verdict on the New Coke affair came from Pepsi-Cola USA's CEO Roger Enrico, who thought Coca-Cola had learned a valuable lesson:

> I think, by the end of their nightmare, they figured out who they really are. Caretakers. They can't change the taste of their flagship brand. They can't change its imagery. All they can do is defend the heritage they nearly abandoned in 1985.[xxii]

And the good news? I think there's still time for a similar Methodist resurgence, especially since they have such a solid spiritual heritage found in Old Methodism. That will only occur, however, by reclaiming and defending John Wesley's original stances on the authority and inerrancy of the Bible.

In contrast to the UMC over the last fifty years, theologically conservative Wesleyan denominations have grown. The Church of

God by two-thirds, the Wesleyan Church by 75%, and the Assemblies of God by a whopping 500%! All three prioritize the inerrancy of Scripture, and none of them are experiencing the same exodus as the United Methodist Church.[xxiii]

There's also encouraging proof of a modern-day United Methodist revival in the works, found in the return to orthodoxy led by Methodists on the African continent:

> Thanks to growing United Methodism in Africa, the denomination as a whole is growing by over 100,000 members annually, with the over 200,000 gain in Africa more than compensating for the U.S. church's nearly 100,000 annual loss. African influence on the U.S.-based bureaucracy will eventually push it in a more orthodox, evangelistic direction. It already has helped transform the General Board of Global Ministries. Inevitably the U.S. seminaries will be positively influenced by a denomination that is soon to be majority African.[xxiv]

As we've learned through the story of New Coke, there's no substitute for the real thing. As a final plea to our Methodist friends: There's no substitute for Scripture. It was originally your first love. Please return to it, your brothers and sisters miss you and need you to stand with us, now more than ever.

Chapter Eight
Puff Graham:
The Stuff of Bible-Believing Legend

"Puff Graham" was all the telegram said. Sent to newspaper and TV outlets throughout the United States, this cryptic, two-word telegram was enough to launch the famed career of a young, energetic, up and coming pastor from the South. The telegram's author was none other than media mogul William Randolph Hearst, Sr. To this day nobody knows exactly why he sent it, other than signaling to his people to write praiseworthy stories about the "Johnny-come-lately" evangelist. The occasion was a 1949 Los Angeles crusade that began on September 25 and was originally scheduled to run for three weeks. Services were held under the big top, two rented circus tents sewn together and affectionately referred to as "The Canvas Cathedral."

A lanky, blond-haired farmer's boy from Charlotte, North Carolina, Billy Graham preached stirring messages with a rapid-fire cadence that helped him to attain and keep his audience's attention. At age 28, he was already naturally captivating, and the media circus promoted him to millions. Thanks to that now famous two-word directive from Hearst, Graham's likeness appeared on national magazine covers including *Time*, *Life*, and *Newsweek*.

But buried deep beneath the headlines was a little-known fact about an event that took place several weeks prior to the historic crusade and just before the meteoric rise of its famed evangelist.

The heated debate over the Bible's integrity, or inerrancy, had been raging between two unmovable sides for decades. Graham was torn when confronted with the harsh reality of having to cast his lot with one side or the other (neutrality guaranteed both sides would be disappointed). It was the 1940s, and conventional wisdom taught that nobody with half a brain could possibly believe all of Scripture, especially considering how many of its teachings did not accord with modern thought.

Additional pressure was applied on Graham from an unsuspecting source—Charles Templeton, a Canadian-born minister who had helped Graham co-found Youth for Christ. Many referred to the co-evangelists as "The Gold Dust Twins," principally due to Templeton, the more dynamic and talented of the duo. After his freshman year at Princeton Theological Seminary, Templeton had grown increasingly wary of Scripture and leaned on Graham to do the same. The crisis of faith Templeton underwent began like this:

> I picked up Thomas Paine's *The Age of Reason*. In a few hours, nearly everything I knew or believed about the Christian religion was challenged and in large part demolished. My unsophisticated mind had no defenses against the thrust of his logic or his devastating arguments.[xxv]

Templeton's doubts later burgeoned into agnosticism, and by the time of his death in 2001, full-blown atheism, as evidenced by his self-entitled autobiography, *Farewell to God*:

> When finally I shook free of Christianity, it was like being born again. I began to see all of life differently. The

things that had once seemed important now seemed trivial. And things I'd never seen the meaning of or the essence of I began to appreciate for the first time.

I oppose the Christian Church because, for all the good it sometimes does, it presumes to speak in the name of God and to propound and advocate beliefs that are outdated, demonstrably untrue, and often, in their various manifestations, deleterious to individuals and to society.

In August of 1949, just weeks before the famous "Puff Graham" telegram, skepticism mounted in Graham's mind too:

The arguments were, that you really couldn't trust the Scriptures...and I began to think well perhaps they're right. Maybe this Bible isn't as authoritative as I thought it was. And I remember how disturbed I was with that because I had always believed in the Bible.

From his article on the *Friends of Justice* blog, Alan Bean shares Graham's interaction with Henrietta Mears and his response to God:

What happened next is the stuff of evangelical legend. Graham had put up a brave front with his Canadian friend, but the confrontation left him stunned. His first instinct was to seek the counsel of Henrietta Mears, the celebrated Bible teacher and evangelical visionary who had founded Forest Home ten years earlier. Bold, confident, and brimming, as always, with evangelical energy, Mears was just the tonic Graham needed. The inerrancy of Scripture was the bedrock of Christianity, she reminded the young evangelist. Undermine that foundation and the whole edifice collapses.

Graham picked up his Bible and wandered alone into the rugged hill country surrounding Forest Home. Spotting an old tree stump by the side of the path, Graham laid down his opened Bible, and began to pray.

"O God! There are many things in this book I do not understand. There are many problems with it for which I have no solution. There are many seeming contradictions. There are some areas in it that do not seem to correlate with modern science. I can't answer some of the philosophical and psychological questions Chuck and others are raising."

Graham fell to his knees.

"Father, I am going to accept this as Thy Word—by faith! I'm going to allow faith to go beyond my intellectual questions and doubts, and I will believe this to be Your inspired Word!"

With these words, Graham felt the Spirit of God flooding his soul. When he addressed the Forest Home audience the following evening, Henrietta Mears knew she was listening to a new man. There was a confidence, a sense of authority to his preaching that was utterly new and powerful.

From that point forward, all of Graham's sermons were peppered with the phrase, "The Bible says...the Bible says...the Bible says...", because "the Bible has its own built in power and the Lord honored it." Graham recognized:

> When I stand before the people and say, 'God says,' or 'The Bible says,' the Holy Spirit uses me. There are results. I don't have the time or the intellect to examine all sides of each theological question, so I've decided, once and for all, to stop questioning and to accept the Bible as God's Word.[xxvi]

Billy Graham's famous Los Angeles Crusade began within two weeks to the day of that tree stump prayer, on the evening of September 25, 1949. Originally scheduled to run two weeks and seat 6,000, plans were hastily adjusted to accommodate the increased demand, adding 3,000 seats and extending the crusade an additional eight weeks.

On November 20, 1949, after the final invitation to accept Christ was offered, a staggering 350,000 people had heard the Gospel at "The Canvas Cathedral," not counting the millions who watched on TV or read their newspapers.

Had it not been for the bold, lion-like resilience of Henrietta Mears (the perfect counterweight to a large opposition), who knows what the world might have missed. For the 215 million attendees who heard Billy Graham preach in person over the course of his life, the answer is quite a lot.

If you have unanswered concerns about your faith or the authority of Scripture, don't be discouraged. So many in churches across the country (and around the world) are feeling the same tension. Even champions of the faith like Billy Graham experienced seasons of questioning!

Healthy dialogue about what we believe and why we believe it is incredibly important. But as you engage with others and seek answers for yourself, be wary of more modern-day Charles Templetons in and among your church, including those in leadership. What can you do in response? Expectantly look for biblical counterweights to culture, like Henrietta Mears or Billy Graham, that support the inerrancy of God's Word. Better yet, dig into the Bible, find the answers, and become that counterweight yourself.

"This is exactly how I
saw it in my head."

Chapter Nine
Where Do We Go From Here?

I have what I believe is a reasonable request, especially in light of the ultra-polarized climate in which we live. In our increasingly divisive culture, I'm asking servants of Christ to stand firm by doing 5 things:

Step One: Ask the Question

Ask and continue asking the question, "Do you believe in inerrancy?" The answers, by the respondent's own admission, will determine in which camp he or she falls and by what ground rules they are playing.

Ambiguity will be removed, just as it is with a true or false statement. Take Psalm 18:30 for instance: "As for God, his way is perfect: The Lord's word is flawless; He shields all who take refuge in him." If someone claims this is false, at least you're off to an honest start in your conversation.

Step Two: Answer the Question

Answer the question, "Does the Christian religion offer a cafeteria plan?" Much like step one above, the answer is either yes or no. With picking and choosing what to believe in the Bible, someone ultimately has to decide what's in and what's out—who wants that responsibility?

Let's quit kidding ourselves—God doesn't need our help making additions or omissions to His Word to make it more appealing. Instead, we should start learning why the Bible is true, regardless of time or culture, and how it applies to everyone.

Step Three: Educate

Shore up your belief system on the Old and New Testaments, then determine how you plan to defend those positions. I've done my best to convince you of the importance of biblical inerrancy, but there's no substitute for digging into the heart of the Word to see for yourself.

> "For whatever was written in earlier times was written for our instruction, so that through perseverance and the encouragement of the Scriptures we might have hope." (Romans 15:4)

Step Four: Pick a Side

Whether we like it or not, the time is coming when we will all have to pick a side. For everyone's sake, please don't muddy the waters by taking the "parts are true, parts aren't" approach to the Bible.

According to Jesus, the absolute last place on earth you'd want to find yourself is the passionless middle (remember Barth?). By Jesus' own account, He regards that space the most egregious of all:

I know your deeds, that you are neither cold nor hot;
I wish that you were cold or hot. So because you are
lukewarm, and neither hot nor cold, I will vomit you
out of My mouth. (Revelation 3:15-16)

There's really only two options—either accept the sufficiency of Scripture or reject 100% of it out of hand.

Step Five: Champion the Cause

"The Bible is God's Word and is absolutely true in every detail. God never errs and neither does His Word. God's Word is 100% true from Genesis to Revelation. Men's ability to find fault with God and His Word is about to run out."

– Pastor Bob Wilkin

According to Pastor Steven J. Cole, the one who rejects God's testimony to His Son through unbelief makes God out as a liar, which is a serious matter. Nobody wants to be called a liar, especially in the context of trying to help someone:

If I offered a poor person a check for $100 and he grabbed me by the lapel and said, "Prove to me that this check is good," I'd have good reason to take my check back and leave him to his misery.

If he ripped my check in two and threw it back at me, he would not experience the blessing I offered him.

If a critic angrily says, "Prove to me that Jesus is the Son of God and I'll believe," he is doing far worse than tearing up my check. He is calling the only true God a liar. He is trampling on the gift of God's Son, Who would forgive all his sins if he would receive Him. God has given more than sufficient testimony to His Son. If you receive that external testimony, God will give you the additional inner testimony that He is true. If you reject His external testimony, you will also lack the internal witness.[xxvii]

I couldn't agree more, which is largely why I wrote this book. If I'm preaching to the choir and you are already convinced of the Bible's accuracy, I urge you to please take up the mantle and help defend it—the Church's vitality depends on it.

But if you aren't fully convinced of Scripture's inerrancy, I pray that this book will have lit a spark within you as to the importance of the issue. Regardless of your position, my hope is that you will continue to seek the answers to your questions. If you look in God's Word, I have no doubt you'll find them.

Chapter Ten
Warning Shots

To our enemy and the culture you've so cunningly deceived. Through incremental changes made in the name of progress and intellectual enlightenment, you've successfully marginalized the Christian faith from relevance.

So many of us have been scolded or punished for adhering to Christianity in its original form. You've insisted we rebrand and adopt a kinder, softer, gentler approach to faith. Somehow you managed to seduce an entire people into asking, "Did God really say..." though one look within the Word makes clear exactly where God stands.

You convinced us that the One and only true God came across as narrow-minded and exclusive, that He must be substituted with a more general higher power. You've convinced so many that the message of repentance and baptism were antiquated. In response, we've replaced God's message with the directive to simply try our best, be a good person, and help others, despite what even one of our most outspoken antagonists could foresee:

> One should notice that Christianity has crossed over into a gentle *moralism*: it is not so much 'God, freedom, and immortality' that have remained, as benevolence and decency of disposition, and the belief that in the whole universe too benevolence and decency of disposition prevail: it is the *euthanasia* of Christianity.
>
> – Friedrich Nietzsche

But that's about to change. Contrary to what you want the masses to believe, people are starving to hear right versus wrong. Moral relativism has grown grossly out of style.

Whether or not they fully understand why, people have grown weary trying to navigate their way through endless mazes of vagueness. As a result your subtle choke-hold on Christianity is loosening. You're losing control. You know it, and so do we.

So to our enemy, and the culture you've so readily deceived—here's what you can expect from God's people going forward.

No More Disclaimers
No more apologizing for our belief in the authority of the Bible as God's Word. Christians tripping over themselves to apologize has always struck me as odd, especially considering how we've experienced Jesus in the realest of ways. "Come and see for yourself" is what our Faith's Founder has to say. What's required is to take a first step towards "a far more excellent way." (1 Cor. 12:31)

Grace and Truth

We are called to be Christlike, and that's exactly what we're going to do. Jesus of Nazareth had the remarkable ability to pair hard truths with unbridled love. In one breath, He could admonish, "Whoever is ashamed of Me and My words, I will be ashamed of him." And in the next breath, implore, "Come to Me, all who are weary and heavy laden, and you will find rest for your souls." The Spirit of Jesus abides within us, and He has enabled us to speak the truth in love, which makes our faith an unstoppable force to be reckoned with.

Back in the Fray

Shame on Bible-believing Christians for retreating from the public sector in the first place. In the interim, we learned a valuable lesson—just as a rising tide can lift all ships, Christians can elevate the public discourse. We will hold fast to the promises found in the Bible and boldly walk them out going forward:

> Aim for perfect harmony, encourage one another, be of one mind, live in peace. And the God of love and peace will be with you. (2 Corinthians 13:11)

We're Getting It Right This Time

Our past hypocrisy is inexcusable. We've left countless lost souls in our wake, but no longer will we continue handing out excuses for denying what is true. Instead, we are inviting others to do as we do, not only as we say. Quite simply, we're changing our ways. Although we've been out of sight and out of mind for ages, we're coming back into view. It's a fascinating time to be a Christian; we can sense it, and so can you.

Frequently Asked Questions

Is inerrancy really that big of a deal?

Absolutely! The Bible stands or falls as a whole. If a major newspaper were routinely discovered to contain errors, it would be quickly discredited. It would make no difference to say, "All the errors are confined to page three." For a paper to be reliable in any of its parts, it must be factual throughout. In the same way, if the Bible is inaccurate when it speaks of geology, why should its theology be trusted? It is either a trustworthy document, or it is not.[xxviii]

Does Biblical inerrancy mean we have to stop using our minds or blindly accept what the Bible says?

No, not by any means. We are commanded to study the Word (2 Timothy 2:15), and those who search it out are commended (Acts 17:11). Also, we recognize that there are difficult passages in the Bible, as well as sincere disagreements over interpretation. Our goal should be to approach Scripture reverently and prayerfully. When we find something we do not understand, we pray harder, study more, and—if the answer still eludes us—humbly acknowledge our own limitations in the face of the perfect Word of God.[xxix]

Does inerrancy allow room for interpretive discussion or disagreement?

Yes—it happens all the time. People with equally high views of the Bible's authority disagree on interpretations of individual texts regularly. The fact that the Bible itself is without error does not mean any one person's interpretations are inerrant. Open and honest dialogue about what passages mean and/or how to apply them is an essential part of faith.

Who wrote the Bible: God or man?

Both. It is accurate to say that God wrote the Bible. According to 2 Timothy 3:16, Scripture is "breathed out" by God. However, saying that God wrote the Bible does not mean He took a pen in hand, grabbed some parchment, and physically wrote the text of Scripture. His "writing" of Scripture was not a physical action on His part. Rather, God's authorship was accomplished through the process of inspiration, as human writers wrote God's message.

So, it is also accurate to say that inspired men of God wrote the Bible. The doctrine of the inspiration of Scripture essentially teaches that God "superintended" the human authors of the Bible so that their individual styles were preserved but the result was precisely what God wanted. When Matthew, for example, sat down to write an account of Jesus' ministry, he relied on his memory (he was an eyewitness to the events he recorded) with help from the Holy Spirit (John 14:26), keeping his intended readership in mind (Matthew wrote for a Jewish audience). The result was the Gospel of Matthew—a narrative full of Matthew's vocabulary, Matthew's grammar, Matthew's syntax, and Matthew's style. Yet it was God's Word. The Spirit had so guided Matthew's writing that everything God wanted to say was said, and nothing was included that God did not intend to say.[xxx]

What does it mean, "only the original autographs are free from error?"

To be inerrant is to be free from error. Only the original autographs (the original manuscripts written by the apostles, prophets, etc.) are under the divine promise of inspiration and inerrancy. The books of the Bible, as they were originally written under the inspiration of the Holy Spirit (2 Timothy 3:16–17; 2 Peter 1:20–21), are 100 percent inerrant, accurate, authoritative, and true. There is no biblical promise that copies of the original manuscripts would be equally inerrant or free from errors. As the Bible has been copied thousands of times over thousands of years, some copyist errors have likely occurred.[xxxi]

If we don't have any original manuscripts in hand, how can we know they are accurate?

We do have an accurate copy of the original text represented in these manuscripts (see Geisler and Nix, GIB, chapter 11);

The nearly 5,800 New Testament manuscripts we possess contain all or nearly all of the original text, and we can reconstruct the original text with over 99 percent accuracy.

To illustrate, were the original U.S. Constitution to be destroyed, we would not lose the constitutional authority for our country, even if all we had were copies with flaws in them. The original could be reconstructed with enough certainty to assure the continuance of our constitutional republic. The same is true of the Bible in our hands. Even though it is based on copies, they are accurate copies that convey to us 100 percent of all essential truths in the original.[xxxii]

Does the Bible contain errors?

As Norman Geisler frames it, human beings, whether scientists or biblical scholars, are finite, and finite beings make mistakes. That is why there are erasers on pencils, correcting fluid for typing, and a "delete" button on keyboards. And even though God's Word is perfect (Psalms 19:7), as long as imperfect human beings exist, there will be misinterpretations of God's Word and false views about His world. None of these prove errors in God's revelations but only errors in our interpretations of them.

When we run into a so-called "error" in the Bible, we must assume one of two things: either the manuscript was not copied correctly, or we have not understood it rightly. What we may not assume is that God made an error in inspiring the original text.[xxxiii]

Is everything in the Bible meant to be taken literally?

No. As a human book, the Bible uses various human literary devices. Several whole books are written in poetic style (e.g., Job, Psalms, Proverbs); the Synoptic Gospels are filled with parables; in Galatians 4, Paul utilizes an allegory; the New Testament abounds with metaphors (e.g., 2 Cor. 3:2–3; James 3:6) and similes (cf. Mat. 20:1; James 1:6); hyperboles may also be found (e.g., Col. 1:23; John 21:25; 2 Cor. 3:2), and possibly even poetic figures (Job 41:1); Jesus employed satire (Mat. 19:24 with 23:24); and figures of speech are common. It is incorrect to assume that all these should be taken literally, thus resulting in contradictions. All of the Bible is literally true, but not all the Bible is true literally (there are symbols and figures of speech too).[xxxiv]

What about science and history?

Some have suggested that Scripture can always be trusted on spiritual and moral matters, but it is not always correct on historical matters. However, these matters are often inextricably interwoven with the historical and scientific. A close examination of Scripture reveals that the scientific (factual) and spiritual truths are often inseparable. For example, one cannot separate the spiritual truth of Christ's resurrection from the fact that His body permanently vacated the tomb and later physically appeared (see Matt. 28:6;

1 Cor. 15:13-19). Likewise, if Jesus was not born of a biological virgin, then He is no different from the rest of the human race on whom the stigma of Adam's sin rests (see Rom. 5:12). Historical reality and the theological doctrine stand or fall together. If one denies that the literal space-time event occurred, then there is no basis for believing the scriptural doctrine built upon it.

Jesus asserted to Nicodemus, "If I told you earthly things and you do not believe, how will you believe if I tell you heavenly things" (John 3:12, NASB)? In short, if the Bible does not speak truthfully about the physical world, then it cannot be trusted when it speaks about the spiritual world. The two are intimately related.[xxxv]

What is the simplest way to describe inerrancy?
God cannot err.
The Bible is the Word of God.
Therefore, the Bible cannot err.

What is the most concise summary statement on inerrancy?

The Chicago Statement on Biblical Inerrancy[xxxvi]

1. God, who is Himself Truth and speaks truth only, has inspired Holy Scripture in order thereby to reveal Himself to lost mankind through Jesus Christ as Creator and Lord, Redeemer, and Judge. Holy Scripture is God's witness to Himself.

2. Holy Scripture, being God's own Word, written by men prepared and superintended by His Spirit, is of infallible divine authority in all matters upon which it touches: It is to be believed, as God's instruction, in all that it affirms; obeyed, as

God's command, in all that it requires; embraced, as God's pledge, in all that it promises.

3. The Holy Spirit, Scripture's divine Author, both authenticates it to us by His inward witness and opens our minds to understand its meaning.

4. Being wholly and verbally God-given, Scripture is without error or fault in all its teaching, no less in what it states about God's acts in creation, about the events of world history, and about its own literary origins under God, than in its witness to God's saving grace in individual lives.

5. The authority of Scripture is inescapably impaired if this total divine inerrancy is in any way limited of disregarded, or made relative to a view of truth contrary to the Bible's own; and such lapses bring serious loss to both the individual and the Church.

Notes

While I do not endorse every opinion held by these authors and sources, I found these sources useful while writing this book. I pray that they and others will also help you during your own research into biblical inerrancy.

i   The Bible was divinely inspired by God, who used over 40 different authors to write it in 3 different languages over a period of 1,500 years!

ii   Though grammatically correct, I've always hated capitalizing the enemy's name. To me, it's not worth being referred to as a "proper" name. All punctuation of satan, devil, enemy, etc. are intentional.

iii   "For just as Jonah was in the stomach of the great fish for three days and three nights, so will the Son of Man be in the heart of the earth for three days and three nights. The men of Nineveh will stand up with this generation at the judgment, and will condemn it because they repented at the preaching of Jonah; and behold, something greater than Jonah is here." (Matthew 12:40-41)

"For the coming of the Son of Man will be just like the days of Noah. For as in those days before the flood they were eating and drinking, marrying and giving in marriage, until the day that Noah entered the ark, and they did not understand until the flood came and took them all away; so will the coming of the Son of Man be." (Matthew 24:37-39)

"And He said to them, 'I was watching satan fall from heaven like lightning.'" (Luke 10:18)

iv   "The Infallibility of Scripture" (Sermon by Charles Spurgeon)

v   Hannah, John D. Inerrancy and the Church. Moody Press, 1984.

vi   Pruess, Robert, and John Girstner. Inerrancy. Zondervan, 1980.

vii   Tabor, Chuck. "When Things Just Don't Add Up." Wilmington News Journal, 15 Oct. 2020, https://www.wnewsj.com/

	news/religion/148721/when-things-just-dont-add-up.
viii	"This hope we have as an anchor of the soul, a hope both sure and reliable and one which enters within the veil," (Hebrews 6:19)
ix	Anecdotally, I hope what happened to Keith following that conversation will project onto the culture at large: a full and complete surrender to Christ, the Captain of his soul.
x	"U.S. Population Growth Rate 1950-2022." MacroTrends, https://www.macrotrends.net/countries/USA/united-states population-growth-rate.
xi	Jones, Rick. "PC(USA) 2021 Statistics Continue to Show Declining Membership." Presbyterian Church (U.S.A.), 25 Apr. 2022, https://www.pcusa. org/news/2022/4/25/pcusa-2021-statistics-contin ue-show-declining-memb/.
xii	Nelson, J. Herbert. "'We Are Not Dying. We Are Reforming.'" Presbyterian Church (U.S.A.), 24 May 2017, https://www.pcusa. org/news/2017/5/24/we-are-not-dying-we-are-reforming/.
xiii	Jones, Rick. "PC(USA) 2021 Statistics Continue to Show Declining Membership." Presbyterian Church (U.S.A.), 25 Apr. 2022, https://www.pcusa.org/news/2022/4/25/pcusa-2021-statistics-continue-show-declining-memb/.
xiv	Mohler, Albert. "The Inerrancy of Scripture: The Fifty Years' War. . .and Counting." Albert Mohler, 16 Aug. 2010, https://albertmohler.com/2010/08/16/the-inerrancy-of-scripture-the-fifty-years-war-and-counting.
xv	Craik, Henry, ed. English Prose. New York: The Macmillan Company, 1916; Bartleby.com, 2010. www.bartleby.com/209/.
xvi	See John Wesley's Explanatory Notes Upon the New Testament.
xvii	UMData: The United Methodist Church Online Directory & Statistics: 2022, http://www.umdata.org/UMFactsHome.aspx.
xviii	The Association of Religion Data Archives: 2012, https://www.thearda.com/Denoms/D_1469.asp.
xix	Tooley, Mark. "Fifty Years Since Methodism Grew in America." The Institute on Religion & Democracy Blog. 28 Jan. 2015, https://juicyecumenism.com/2015/01/28/fifty-years-since-methodism-grew-in-america/.
xx	Stark, Rodney. What Americans Really Believe: New Findings from the Baylor Surveys of Religion (Waco: Baylor University Press, 2008) p. 4.
xxi	Ibid.
xxii	others, K. Fogarty and. "New Coke." Encyclopedia Britannica,

	Aug. 13, 2018. https://www.britannica.com/topic/New-Coke.
xxiii	Tooley, Mark. "Fifty Years Since Methodism Grew in America." The Institute on Religion & Democracy Blog. 28 Jan. 2015, https://juicyecumenism.com/2015/01/28/fifty-years-since-methodism-grew-in-america/.
xxiv	Ibid.
xxv	Bean, Alan. "Billy Graham's Shadow: Chuck Templeton and the Crisis of American Religion." Friends of Justice Blog, 12 Jan. 2020.
xxvi	Ibid.
xxvii	Cole, Steven J. "Lesson 23: Is Christianity Merely Psychlogical? (1 John 5:6-13)." Bible.org, 2006, https://bible.org/seriespage/lesson-23-christianity-merely-psychological-1-john-56-13.
xxviii	Ibid.
xxix	Ibid.
xxx	Ibid.
xxxi	Ibid.
xxxii	Geisler, Norman. Systematic Theology, Vol. 1, Introduction, Bible, Bethany House Publishers, 2002.
xxxiii	Ibid.
xxxiv	Ibid.
xxxv	"The Inerrancy of the Bible." The North American Missions Board, 30 Mar. 2016, https://www.namb.net/apologetics/resource/the-inerrancy-of-the-bible/.
xxxvi	The Chicago Statement on Biblical Inerrancy." Alliance of Confessing Evangelicals, https://www.alliancenet.org/the-chicago-statement-on-biblical-inerrancy. Why Is It Important to Believe in Biblical Inerrancy?"GotQuestions.org, 9 Feb. 2007, https://www.gotquestions.org/Biblical-inerrancy.